...turn on or before the last date s...ed be'  da

# Just one more job

## by Ann Ruffell

D1336161

AXIS education

Rotherham College of Arts and Technology

R53560

## Acknowledgements

**Cover design:** Oliver Heath, Rafters Design

**Illustrations on pages 5, 7, 9, 11, 13, 15, 17, 21, 23, 27, 29 and 31 © Paul Gardiner, 2005.** The right of Paul Gardiner to be identified as the illustrator of this work has been asserted by him in accordance with the Copyright, Design and Patents Act, 1988.

Brinsford books are a direct result of the findings of a two-year authoring/research project with young offenders at HMYOI Brinsford, near Wolverhampton. Grateful thanks go to all the young people who participated so enthusiastically in the project and to Judy Jackson and Brian Eccleshall of Dudley College of Technology.

**Copyright © Axis Education 2005**

All rights reserved; no part of this publication my be reproduced, stored in a retrieval system, transmitted in any form, or by any means, electronic, mechanical, photocopying, recording, or otherwise, without the prior written permission of the publisher.

First published in Great Britain by Axis Education Ltd

ISBN 1-84618-004-x

Axis Education PO Box 459
Shrewsbury SY4 4WZ

Email: enquiries@axiseducation.co.uk

www.axiseducation.co.uk

Martin walked out of the gate.

He was a free man.

Prison was behind him now. He had done 18 months. He did not want to do any more.

They had been okay in there.

He had done classes. He had papers to prove it. He could get a job.

He was going to go straight this time.

He looked around.

Where was Mum?

She said she would come to meet him but she was not here. He looked at his watch. It was the right time. Perhaps she had missed the bus.

They had given him a bit of money. It was okay for a bus, not for a taxi.

But there was a guy in a car. He pulled up.

"Hey, Mart! Come on!" It was his mate from way back. Martin was glad to see his mate. But he ought to keep away if he wanted to go straight.

FCFS

LIBRARY & LEARNING
RESOURCES CENTRE

Acc. No. R 53560
2/3/06 P
CLASS: FIC R

"Den! What you doing here?" He shook Den's hand.
"Your Mum said to come and get you," said Den.
"Why? Why is Mum not with you?" It was odd. Mum had come to visit him every time. She never missed.
"Don't you know?" said Den. "You have got a new Dad."

Martin felt gutted. His Mum had not told him.
She had come all those times but had not told him about a new Dad.
He had a bad feeling about this.

"Don't come in," he said to Den when they got home.
"I'll see you."
"You want anything, you only have to ask," said Den.
"Right, mate. Thanks."
And Martin walked back into his home.

It was nearly as bad as he thought.
His new Dad was big and stocky.
Martin could see that if it came to a row he would lose.
And he could see that there would be lots of rows.

The first thing his new Dad said was,

"If you want to stay here you must do what I say.

I don't want your sort here."

He would not let Martin's mum stick up for him.

Martin went to see his girlfriend.

Lucy would be there for him.

Always had been.

She was a star.

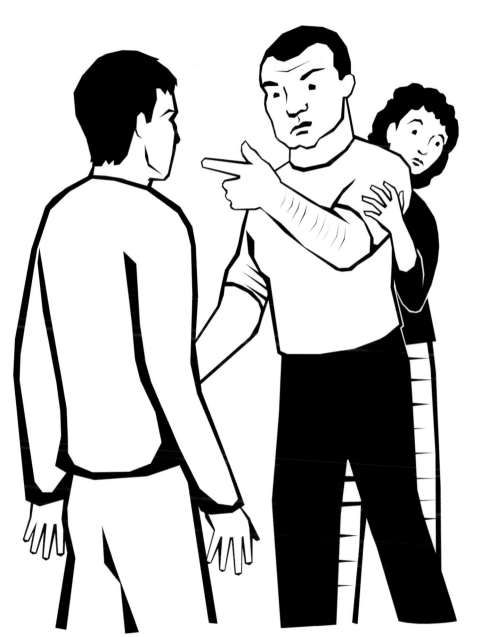

But it was the same with Lucy.

She had been to visit, while he was in the nick. But all the time she was seeing this new guy.

"Sorry, Mart. I am really sorry."

Maybe she was, but it did not help him.

"I have got a spare room," said Den.

"You could come and stay here."

Martin was angry. "Right, I will," he said.

"But I have not got any money."

"Easy," said Den. "You are good at car radios, right?
I have a nice little thing going.
Easy to pass them on. Good money."
"No," said Martin. "I am going straight."

"Suit yourself," said Den. "But you have got to live."
Den was right. He had to live.
It was his mum's fault. She should not have shacked up
with this man. He could have gone home. He could
have made a good thing of his life. But she had let him
down.

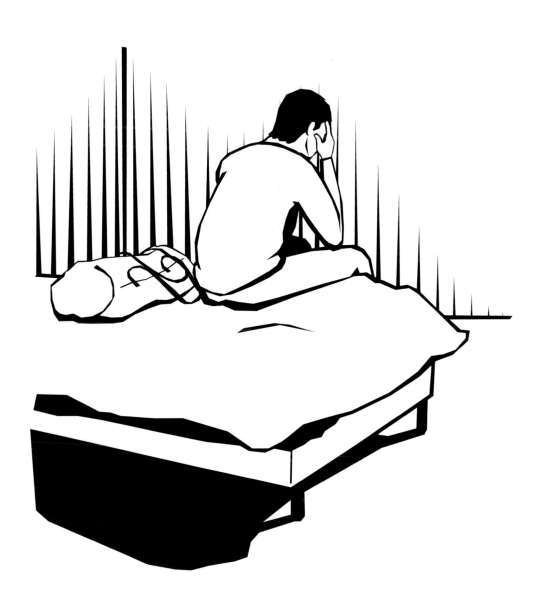

"Okay, Den," he said. "Show me."

They were little things at first. A few cars, a few car radios. It made a bit of money.

But they could not sell the stuff straight on. They had to go through a middle man. There had to be a better way.

"Sod this," said Den. "If we snatch money it will be all ours. Nobody else has to take a cut."

"There is lots of stuff out there on the street," agreed Martin. "The way people carry cash around, they are asking for it."

He wanted to buy a good car. Den had a cool Astra GTE.

They watched people bringing cash to pay in to banks. It would be easy. Run, grab, run again.

They did not see the cop car that pulled out of a side road. Not until the blue lights came up behind them.

"Go on the main road and miss them between the traffic."

Traffic was heavy. It should be easy to blow the cops.

Den was a good driver. He spun the car round and made for the town. A bike was in the way. Martin yelled at the guy out of the window.

The cops got stuck behind a bus.

Den drove fast the other way. They parked the car and ran.

The guys had not taken much that day. The bag was full of coins.

"Shit!" said Den. "We nearly got nicked for that! It is not worth it."

"Too much stress for too little," said Martin. "We might as well do one big job to get big cash. Then we don't need to do any more."

"We need more people for that," said Den. "I will get Karl on the phone."

They were going to rob an off-licence. A proper hold-up this time.

Karl said they had to get a gun. "You cannot do a good job without a gun," he said.

He got one from a crack dealer that he knew.

Den gave the gun to Martin. "Look after that," he said.
Martin did not want the gun. He had never used a gun
before.

"Just keep it safe," said Den.

But where was a safe place? The only place he could
think of was in the park. Down in the ground.

Martin went out at night. He took a shovel, the sort you
use for coal.

He had a plastic bag for the gun and the shovel. It
looked as if he had just been to buy some cans.

The park was locked. He climbed over the wall.

He heard a noise. It made him jump.

But it was only a fox.

The park did not look the same at night. He had to choose a good place. He would have to remember the place again.

In the daytime too many people went by the lake.

The tennis courts were always full.

The play park was empty now, but tomorrow it would be full of kids and mums.

The toilets stank. There were people there even at night. Other people had climbed over the wall. They were using crack.

That would be no good.

He had to get away from there.

Then he found the best place. It was right where nobody ever went.

There were new trees and a new fence.

He dug a deep hole and put the gun in it. Then he hid the shovel in the bushes.

Karl would get a car. He was the driver this time. Den would be at the door.

"You have got the gun," said Den. "You must be the one to go in."

It would be his last job, and then he could go straight.

The night before the job Martin went to the park. He climbed over the fence.

The crack users were over by the toilets but there was no one by the new trees.
His shovel was still there.
So was the gun, still in its bag.

Karl had nicked a good car. It could move off fast.
They drove to the off-licence.
It was time to put on their masks.
"Quick, now!" said Den.
Martin felt the gun in his pocket. He ran inside.

They were lucky. There was no one in the shop. Only the man on the till.

"Don't move," said Martin. He pointed the gun. "Open the till and take out the cash. Slowly."
"You bastard!" said the man. But he had to hand over the cash. Martin grabbed it and ran.

Den had the car door open. They were off in five seconds.

Back home they counted up the cash.

"That's less than £85 each," said Den.

Martin could not go straight with only £85.

"Not worth all that stress," said Karl. "We must go for something bigger. Like a supermarket. My girlfriend works in Kwiksave."

They went to see Jo.

She told them how things worked in Kwiksave.

"Come in and see," she said. "I can show you where things are."

They went to case the job. They could get the boxes from the front. Or they could get the manager in his office.

Jo told them what time the Securicor van came.

"The manager has all the cash in his office then," she said.

"That will be the best plan," said Martin.

"We'll need one more lad for this," said Karl. "Someone must watch for the Securicor van. We have to be there before it comes."

Sol had done this kind of job before. He told them the best way. This time they all had guns.
Even Karl had one this time.

The manager was scared. He did not have time to hit the panic button. Martin made the manager hand over all the cash. It was a doddle. Den and Sol covered him. A girl screamed, but they soon stopped her.

Karl nearly hit the Securicor van. The man in the van waved his fist. He did not know they had robbed the shop.

"Bad!" said Sol. He was well chuffed.
Karl screamed round the corners. They were home before the cops had any idea.

It took a long time to count the money. They had made
£10,000. Even between four it was a good haul.
But it was still not enough for Martin to go straight.
He had forgotten he had done classes in jail.
He had forgotten the papers he had.
He had forgotten that once he wanted a job.

"One more job, man, and we are set up for life,"
said Sol.

They talked about it. It had to be a big one.
"Then we can live good and no more worries,"
said Martin.
"The Securicor depot," said Karl. "That is where the
cash is. We will do the job there."

It took a lot of planning. They were not in a hurry. They had cash for clubs and girls and other stuff.

They watched the depot.

They noted the times the vans went in and out.

They did not know they were on CCTV.

The police saw them watching the depot. The cops began to watch them.

On the day of the job it looked like all was well.
The plan was good. They had it all worked out.
Karl had nicked a really good car for their getaway.
They drove to the depot.

"Masks on," said Karl. He lit a fag and stood by the car.
It was warm, ready to go.

The police were ready too. The lads had no idea.
They had been lucky so far. But today their luck had run
out. Sol was at the door. Martin and Den went in.
It looked good. All went to plan.
They even had their hands on the cash.

Then the police busted them.

"Hands up!" yelled the cops.

Sol fired his gun. Den and Martin dropped the cash and ran.

Where was Karl? The rat had gone!
Den and Martin turned and fired in the air.
They wanted to scare the cops.
The cops fired back.
Sol got out but Den fell.
Red blood spread on the floor.

Martin could not run.
His best mate had been killed.
It had been one job too many.